That so-easy thing
Rosie Shepperd

smith|doorstop

Published 2012 by
Smith/Doorstop Books
The Poetry Business
Bank Street Arts
32-40 Bank Street
Sheffield S1 2DS

ISBN 978-1-906613-72-3
Typeset by Utter
Printed by People for Print, Sheffield

Acknowledgements

Acknowledgements are due to editors of the following magazines/
anthologies in which some of these poems first appeared: *Agenda*, *Ambit*,
Bow-Wow Shop, Seren (*Foundlings Anthology*), *Oxonian Review*, *Poetry
Ireland*, *Poetry London*, *Rialto*, Cinnamon Press (*A Roof of Red Tiles*).
'Tomorrow will be a day beloved of your father and of you' won the Ted
Walters/Liverpool University prize in 2009 and has been commended in
the 2012 Hippocrates Poetry Competition. 'What I need, Bernard, is a
bit of notice' was commended in the 2008 Manchester Poetry Prize. 'It's
no good' was commended in the 2009 Ware and Norwich Café Writers
competitions.

Thanks

I am deeply grateful for the unstinting support of all the supervisors and
students on Glamorgan University's creative writing programme and to
the inspirational Anne-Marie Fyfe.
With love and thanks to the best readers and friends Liane Strauss and
Lucy Ingrams.

Smith/Doorstop Books are a member of Inpress:
www.inpressbooks.co.uk. Distributed by Central Books Ltd., 99 Wallis
Road, London E9 5LN

The Poetry Business is an Arts Council National Portfolio Organisation

Contents

for Pete, Sam and Georgie

Thoughts inside a rented silver Opel

The day we visit Portofino, I get sick,
        lie in the car,
           in the back,
                in the shade of a eucalyptus.
    The footfalls of couples,
        perhaps families, flap down the hill
           to the sea.
    Their voices flutter.
        "Are you hungry or shall we explore?"
    "Look at the boats. They're so, just so."
        "I know. It's beautiful, isn't it?"
Others look at the water like it's one more thing they don't get.
They say stuff like, "Why did you drink so much last night?"
           Or, "You know I don't" and
               "It doesn't matter any more."
I know I'm sick because I sleep
    in the middle of the day, in our hired Europcar that smells of
        cleaning fluid and has no dust,
           no dust anywhere.
   You tap on the window,
        hold up a Fanta with a spinning pink straw.
           "How're you feeling, Baby?"
You show me a few pieces of smooth white shell.
    We collect them from our sandals,
        our curled up towels, our underwear
    at the end of a day at the beach.
Whatever happens, I don't want to miss anything.

A weekend alone in Paris makes no difference at all

The rattling lift at the Hotel St Boniface,
                              my too-tight new shoes,
               turn left into Rue de Médicis,
move towards the lake, the children in tartan coats, their battleships.
       Bretagne, Lorraine, Foudre; the undefeated Fantasque.

                    It was warmer yesterday at the Tuileries.

                    Light chairs rest on the gravel,
               Table tops are marked from glass tulips of eaux de vie:

Kirsch. Poire. Framboise.

                    The air moves as a man passes.
       I catch the darkness of his coat, the oyster blue of his scarf.
He doesn't turn, doesn't slow down, doesn't change pace.
               I want to say it doesn't matter. It isn't you.
       It does matter. They are all you.

Just my own dumb self
(Raymond Carver – Ultramarine)

I think it was a Tuesday, back
        in my oranger days, when
there was so much to do.
        The kids were sick – nothing bad;
fever and throat mostly.
        We ran out of some thing and I
forgot to collect something else.
        A thump and the boiler died.
A ring and the phone called
        to say someone's mother
was about to have a bad day.
        Ten minutes here, five over there.
But each tiny slot yielded
        something. These days, thin
hours float past, without touching
        into something like entropy.
With just my own dumb self
        for company, the pages are white
and I am cold. Even when the left
        curtain blows its flowered pattern
across my desk, a boy shouts
        Hey and lays a blue bike on a patch
of cut grass. Even when
        the refrigerator starts to hum
it's little white song; stops when I listen.
        Hums. Then stops. Nothing.

Je Reviens

They say, "He can't hear and he can't see; he won't know you're you.
Did you hear? Mrs B set fire to her bed and put it out with her tea."

That you? He says, as I know he will, and, *Is that the new perfume?*

I brush my wrist across his cheek, he sniffs and smiles a bit too.
Did I buy it for you on a trip? A trip to The Great Antilles?

He hears a little, he sees a little, he knows that I'm in his room.

I think I remember now, he says, *was the bottle round and blue?*
Under his sheet is a boy of twelve, not a man of eighty-three.

That you? He says, as I know he will, and, *Is that the new perfume?*

A nurse called Kingston bathes him and brings us all the news
in a voice of sun on summer rain on the slopes of Blue Hills Peak.

He can't hear well, he can't see well. I bring the Peak to his room.

This morning a lady of ninety goes out in her cardie and shoes,
she makes her way to the motorway in a fuss as the post hasn't been.

That you? He says, as I know he will, and, *Is that the new perfume?*

Violet, jasmine, bergamot. Amber, clove and musk. At 72
my father returned to the Antilles, his eyes more milk than blue.

They say he can't hear and he can't see. I know he knows I'm me.
That you? He says, as I know he will, and, *Is that the new perfume?*

Tomorrow will be a day beloved of your father and of you

My name is Dr Seth; we have not met but I know your sister.
I'm going to tell you what we will do now for your father.
He is comfortable, not in pain and has just finished a glass
of apple juice. When I stopped by to see him, he waved
and you know, this may be a good time for you to leave.
You'll be all right, get something to eat, just something light.

I know your mother would much rather drive in daylight.
It's understandable and she is lucky to have you two sisters
close by. You'll be all right. Let's walk. See the leaves;
they have so many colours. The birch by your father's
room – see, see how the branches move, almost in waves
of gold and silver with lamb-tails brushing against the glass.

The sun is low now; there is just time to visit the glass-
houses which, Fr Michael says, are the real highlight
of St Simon's, with their tomatoes, anemones and waves
of vines. You'll be all right. We have time; the lay-sisters
will know where to find us and if he is sleeping, your father,
well, he is sleeping and we must make sure he leaves

us in peace. It will help you to be outside, to leave
that place. See the late sun. Look at the weatherglass.
Tomorrow will give us a day beloved of your father
and of you and feel, even in this precious Autumn light
that is almost too thin, there is life, in you and your sister.
It's all right. See the night-shift in the car park, waving

to their husbands, their wives. They talk in soft waves,
they think of the evening to come, how it will leave
them. Do you know Tagore, the Indian poet? Your sister
brought a book. It's not what you expect, no? The glass
helped your father to read. *Faith is a bird, feeling the light.*
It's all right. I know, you're shocked. A man like your father?

That is what you are thinking, is it not? My father,
reading poems about faith? Tagore is not on his wave-
length, no? Let me tell you. Tagore is a man who delights
all men. Did you know he met Einstein? They both leave
each of us with the idea that we look at life through glass.
It's all right; *chance has its way*, just as you and your sister

have each other. *Chance and causality move together* in waves.
See the lay-sisters; they do not know where the birch leaves fall
or why the lamb-tails brush with such lightness against the glass.

On trying to fathom why I will no longer eat octopus

It's not just the way they're killed;
                    that's just local fishermen exercising their skill,
        although there's a chance that catching octopus
                    might be thought a sport, where men and boys take
    gummy bets on Friday nights and roll cigarettes
                    in dirty hands and flick sharp smiles over yards of meat
    spilling pink from scratched tin scales.

        If hunting's just a hobby, the guts of the problem lie
    in the actions of the mother octopi. Now I may have misunderstood
                    but it seems octopus babies grow in and around
        their neighbourhood, with Mama feeding them
                            (as it were) from herself.
            At this or any other rate, as she gets smaller they get bigger
                and when she feels her hungry opus threatened, her over-reach
rown in her teeth, so to speak, she panics.

        She shoots her sac and moves like shit and through the black,
            one thing's clear; this last ditch effort thins her thinned
    resources and unless the real and/or imagined danger gives up the ghost,
                    she rolls over like a tug. All that investment,
            that titanic struggle, just so we can sit around pretending
    we're not tourists, thinking we know what we're talking about,
                snacking on Sannakji, or Polbo á Feira or Miruhulee Boava.

I tend to tug when I shouldn't even push

From my 30cm table in the café at the Dulwich Picture Gallery.
            I watch your Discovery back into the hellebore,
de-clutch before the ignition dies,
        alarm the estate agent who is enjoying a glance
                over someone's bottom.

The salad of the day is dolphin-friendly-tuna and I know
        you will tell me what this means.
The soup is artichoke and mustard seed.
                The cake is Tuscan Polenta with a Raspberry Coulis.

    You said you had some news.
            I'm not so sure and catching
                    your eye behind your eye,
        I know you're not sure.

Telling me may be too much and
                    on many levels, I wish
            we'd gone for the Indian Summer Grill in College Gardens.

Eyjafjallajökull

One thing I won't do till you get back
                    is sleep on my right side.
            (The other is sleep on my left.)

I'll work through. I'll work till you get back.
        A frenzy of work – productive, creative, expansive, joyful
    (maybe not joyful) but productive,
                            creative and the rest.

        People who come near me at this time will turn away,
almost afraid (or really afraid),
                    afraid of interrupting this passionate outflow.

That's right. It'll be passionate (unlike room-mates
                    or camping equipment or staples).
        When I'm complete, done, replete, spent (you get it),
my hair will be wonderfully unruly and sheets, yes sheets of paper

        will swim about my feet. My upper lip will shimmer
                    with beads – no, droplets of sweat and I will be quiet,
reasonably still and maybe just a little flushed.

You should know that, from the moment of that first
            eruption, earth tremors of greater (and heightened)
                    intensity, are inevitable.

A seedy narrative or moments of lyrical stillness?

A stationery salesman seizes a little extra with
a girl on a summer job in Healthy Snax. You may
consider this anticipated but, you see, he did not
plan to look twice at the pale pink of her easy-wash

overall. And his hand did not intend to brush hers as
she counted his 17p change. But maybe she surprised
him by licking her finger to select a small bag for his
Mexican wrap, pre-packed date slice and grape crush.

Did she experience a premonition of Room 149 at
the Ramada Hotel, just off the Ring Road? Did she
feel a gathering, only that morning as her brothers
jostled like beagles, shovelling toast down the path?

Perhaps he lingered over 2-nights pre-paid or maybe
her pulse quickened at the inclusion of a lemon wedge
in the Friday Fish Special. I'd like to think she paused
at some unexpected warmth. Was it the peach towels?

The sweet circular soap? A delicacy in the afternoon
light from the fly-over? Did she lift the single mint-
chocolate from her pillow, break it in two and save
each half for some tender moment, later?

Much later.

All at length are gathered in

God bless Janet's home-made earrings and alopecia;
>   her marsupial style of eating vol-au-vents.

Creepy Graham rushes from space to space, like a man
>   who has never been invited to anything.

He slides toward my ear, his cheek on mine like a weak
>   blancmange in a freezer bag.

He whispers with toe-curling reverence and cress on his teeth,
>   how much Dad would have loved it. "A day like today!"

Janet eases past the Wilsons, with a plate of salmon pin-wheels,
>   to put one hand on my arm.

"I don't think he'd have really enjoyed his cremation, Graham,
>   whatever the weather."

I stack sandwich plates, pick two cups from the billiard table,
>   shove my head into the study.

A napkin is rolled up on the windowsill that needs a Ronseal;
>   the varnish has splintered and the light is surprising.

Of course, the clocks have gone back, so from here I can pick out
>   pale pieces of pastry, a smudge of béchamel.

The fax machine has a sherry glass beside it with a semi-circle
>   of cerise around the rim. Beverly.

Father Campbell is keen and small, says he wants people to join in
>   at any level; actually says that, then says it again.

He sent me a text on the order of service. He has a business card
and a hatch-back. I ask if the Vatican has

broadband and he reaches for his Sauvignon with a slender left
hand. "Yes. And pay as you go."

I want to think you'll make a neat job of confiscating my heart

It's up to you, but here's an idea.
                                    It could be not dissimilar
                    to the removal of Anne Boleyn's head.
          When he saw the neatness of her muslin cap,
                              and the whiteness of her neck,
the executioner hesitated, called
          fetch my sword to distract them both.
He dispatched her
          before she could gather
                                        anything.

I may feel foolish but I am not unwise.
          Your perception of pain is not unlike garden furniture
                                        left out past September.
          It assumes infinite tolerance to seasons,
                              the reversible effects of corrosion,
                    the garrulous nature of slugs.
                    I know your concentration will be
                                        dipping now,
                    so before you start, I promise:
          There will be no untidiness and it will make
                                        almost no noise.

2 out of 12 organic eggs are cracked;

I feel you might have had a hand in this.
And by the way, these groceries are disastrously packed.

Meat juice in the icing sugar forms a dozen specks
or blobs of brownish red, congealed in sucrose mist
and 4 of 12 organic eggs are cracked.

Pretending to recall means trying to forget
the order of things, although it's pretty hard to miss
these disastrous groceries I guess you must have picked.

2 croissants, 2 peaches; for God's sake just accept
time away from me is time you've missed
the cracks in 6 of these 12 eggs, and yes, they're black.

6 cracked, 2 smashed, 2 breaking, only 2 intact;
hopeful handfuls, holding clear albumen mist.
They sit amidst these groceries (unpacked but not unpicked).

I wait till Sunday morning before I finally crack.
A tiny pause to write a note that reads more like a list:
"These eggs aren't fine; they're yours and all of them are cracked.
These groceries are mine and they're beautifully packed."

How d'ya like them apples?

And then of course, there was the incident
> with a trout; that three pound Paperbelle,
> I pulled from Lake Superior, while you were running for salmon.

I just loved it – the catching of it and the thing itself.
> Luxurious in its brown and gold skin, like that beautiful handbag
> I should've purchased instead of a plane ticket.

The delicious boy with the blue charter boat and the white smile;
> he laughed with me as his nets uncoiled their orangey knots
> and he knelt with me on the hopelessly wet deck to cradle
the trout; my feathery trout with eyes that shone like nothing ever had.

I stayed out on the blue boat, stayed out all afternoon;
> came back to the quay with empty hands and salt in my hair.

> Some things cannot be explained; some creatures
> swim and breathe and cannot be caught.

Somewhere I read that a thought can be exaggerated,
while an emotion cannot

The chef at Suntory considers sea-bream for (maybe) ten seconds.
He selects yellow-fin with absurd red flesh,
smiles at the silver scales;
the dark lines on her back
smile back.

You're late and I flick through The Trib, spy a piece on fish scales.
They grow flat, only on skin;
in the lab they form prisms.
Beyond any meaningful depth,
3D is unnecessary and unhelpful.

It's gone again, that so-easy thing we had for each other.

Unwrapping chopsticks takes forever. I reach for the gold hoshi oki,
you lean yours against your plate,
watch as a sous-chef with extraordinary hands
mixes fine green wasabi with Tokusen;
folds shavings of pink ginger into tiny glazed bowls.

Strangers sit opposite us and next to us, and we incline our heads
together and at each other, bound by this thing,
this art form we're watching. Water chestnuts become flowers, strips
of squid are stencilled, fanned into a helix of white,
thrown into clouds of sesame.

Don't worry; the toughest question is not aimed at you.

What is the name of the thing I call Love?
   (i.m Fanny Nelson née Nisbet, Nisbet's Plantation, Nevis, WI)

Awake at 6.30, looking through the shutters into the black
      green shade of the tamarind.
I have an hour or more and surely
            time beside the ocean will help me find words that are not,
            You would love this.

The elephant grass grows warm, but holds back some
                              part of the night.
            I understand this.
      I know about the calabash and the coconuts and the palms,
            why they were planted in avenues, fifteen feet apart.

      A man in a loose blue shirt
moves across the sand, leans on a rake, lifts his face to The Narrows.
      He walks towards the pontoon, bumping in a breeze;
                        stays still for barely a moment,
            then disappears.

      I sit close to the edge of the beach and wonder
            if Nelson's young wife ever stopped someone in this garden to ask,
                  Who planted that succulent that grows near the sea?
            Does it have a name that might mean something?
            And what is the name of the thing I call Love?

Ponte Vecchio

Not for the first time, I'm staying in a hotel whose name I don't know.
The voice that said I'd join you in Florence? I'm sure that was mine.
But who's this, in a thin blue silk dress, in the thick part of evening?

A long grilled pepper floats in red juices; crazy with oil and sweet basil.
You lean back to tell me, "These places have so many possibilities."
They might be living their possibilities. Not everything is conditional.

My napkin is a starched square, lovely smelling in ceramic neatness.
The round half litre of Morellino sits, patient, to the left of my hand.

You excuse yourself to check on something – It could be anything:
Cheese? Tickets for tomorrow? The faltering signal on your phone?

A flat-faced woman passes, with roses wrapped in cellophane tubes.
It's been a while now since I've stopped making regular use of similes.

The girl you saw

wasn't me. That girl crossed over Piccadilly, wearing tan
Roman sandals, a white shirt, drawn tight on a full blue
skirt. That girl who carried the scent of gardenias, her lips

smiling a colour that isn't deliberate. That wasn't me. That
girl had amber eyes; she whistled top C for a cab and waved
to the man who delivers on a Yamaha bike. It wasn't me who

spread a tapestry shawl on the grass in Green Park, unpacked
pippins and bread, spiced meat and cheap wine. You notice
she waited for no one, threw grapes in the air and sank sharp

teeth, deep into a picnic for one? That girl, she slept full stretch
in the sun, her hand in the pages of *Bonjour Tristesse*. I'd never
read that, not outside, not a slim book that might make me cry.

I've never wiped my face with the front, then the back of my
hand. That girl, she laughed out loud at herself, made an old
Viennese couple jump round and try to join in her day. Did you

see her stand quite still with her arms held high for ten or twelve
seconds? She packed up her things with the smallest of smiles
and glanced down at her watch, the watch I don't wear. You see

it couldn't have been me who pushed a curl of thick hair from
her face and strolled with no map towards Devonshire Gate,
licking two then three fingers; brushing small traces of salt and

white flour from her chin and her cheeks. What did I tell you?
What did I never I tell you? Know this: You could have dreamt
of this girl as me but you've never lived in her dreams as you.

Santa Claus is Leaving Town

That's it. That's all he said. "Cheerio."
Not easy, with an oxygen mask.
That thing.
That thing. Its smugness, the thickness of the plastic, the way it pretended
to be friendly. User friendly.
It doesn't get much worse than Dad's face, under a mask,
leaning up to be kissed.
His poor face,
the tips of his ears pushed down,
the baby skin behind them
rubbed red.
All I had was cleansing pads, the kind I used
to make snowy cuffs on Sam's Santa costume.
The other mothers had laughed.
Little Sam with rows of cleansing pads
tacked at his wrists, around his drooping scarlet hat;
his black boots, too large, the toes
stuffed with socks.
Everything is an improvisation.
With my left hand I hold my father's head,
place torn up cleansing pads
down the sides of his ears,
between skin and savage black elastic.
What I'd give to have him back.
What I'd give to save him from this.

Sleeping lions, go on three.
                              One, two, three,
                                        go sleeping lion.

for my sister

We agreed to go on three,
                    held hands,
                         only not stretched out like kids at the baths.
              Close, like the women we imagined we'd be.

That was the first time
              I looked at our
                    similar hands.
       Not the same.
              We use them in different ways.
                    You hold your cup
                         with both hands.
I loop my index finger around the handle; there's a smooth
              patch of skin there.

That evening, your hands were white.
                    Cold.
I took them, waited, wanting your tiny blood vessels
                    to open up.
       I don't think they did.

What I could not do was leave.
Even when the nurse said, "It is time for you to go now,
              we'll take care of your father."
                    Then, "Think what he would want you to do."
He loved it when we stayed over.

25

I'm sorry. We'd agreed but,
>   I stood, keeping my eyes open to him
>   just in case.

Sleeping lions, go on three.
>   One, two, three.

>   Go.
>   One,
>   two,
>   three.
>   Go, sleeping lion.

I start to understand yellow
  (For Grand-maman)

when I unfold your recipe for soufflé; feel the sweet brittle paper.
        Rosehill, Mauritius, 1938. These ingredients are not possible.
Verna lemons, Suffolk eggs. It's all right. I understand; only the sugar
            made sense on the plantation between Floreal and Beau Bassin.

Some said Grand-papa loved the east of the island and the stretch
            of water facing Rodrigues, across the Arabian Sea to Goa.
It all started there with his curious, grey-eyed mother.

Others said he was a bastard who pissed it all away in a poker shack
            with a mulatto woman from north-west of Souillac.
No-one told her, when he burst through the windscreen of his Jensen
            on a skin-full of Green Island, when the moon was less than.

For fourteen nights she sat with a bundle of children, on a grass hill
            outside Floreal and each night Grand-maman passed silver
casuarinas, holding a warm clay dish of chicken and cardamom rice.

It's no good;

I can't get the fat off my hands even though
           I'm up to my elbows in hot water that has started
                to look like milk.
                        I don't want to think of detergent,
        effluent and the state of my drains.
It must be harissa that clings to my skin
                     in streaks of oily scarlet.
          A heavy lamb shank seemed a fine idea,
     basted with last week's Multipulciano,
          perched on a goo of onions, sugared with rosemary needles.

I hate to look out from the kitchen in the evening.
     The house over there is mostly black with one
                            square of light near the top.
                    It's a bedroom. Her name is Clover.
             She is reading her book for
                       tomorrow.
                 She will turn off the nightlight herse
        When I see the whiteness of her forearm
            extend to the lamp-shade, I know
                I have never seen anyone this brave.

To Rome

Palazzo di Marsciano, August

And when you walked back through the main square at Cortona
did you linger at Café Viola or the smaller one close to the station;
the one with green doors and a dozen tin tables under an awning?

     The tall fair waiter from Croatia; did he signal a space
     by the window, where almonds shine under glass domes?
     Did you taste one or two of the golden cantucci?

Perhaps it seemed too soon for Vin Santo and I wonder,
do you still call it ice wine? My trick was always to stay
for an hour, to enjoy that smooth unfolding of dusk.

     The second hour changed pace and with it the heat
     and the noise of the station crawled from the pavement.
     And men passing through took more from me than my gaze.

That was the time when the light left the day and left me, when
I wanted to stand outside frayed talk of my unlikely return; closer
to the scent of just fading rain as the slow train moved south to Rome.

Perfect and private things have imperfect and public endings
i.m Weldon Kees

And did you chose those friends with care and intelligence and did
they rinse your socks, let out the pinkish water and find a good home
for your cat whose name, I know, is Lonesome? I've read that suicides
prepare themselves with excruciating care, seldom leave errands for
others and yes, I remember they remove their glasses, sometimes
watches and also shoes. They do not tend to empty savings accounts;
usually they eschew talk of starting afresh, anew or anything ridiculous.

I hope your mind has ceased to flap like a broken blind; perhaps it was
broken. Perhaps it is. It may be dawn before you sleep and the silence
of these altered rooms has thinned. I want to think you are there now,
sitting in a different porch-light, where the wind doesn't rush and tall
angular trees are actual and take no holiday. The music will start again
inside a small responsive smile. For a while anyway, let this be enough.